Lee Canter's

Managing the Morning Rush

Shaping Up Your Family's Morning Routine

Lee Canter's Effective Parenting Books

Written by Patricia Sarka and Marcia Shank
Designed by Bob Winberry
Illustrations by Patty Briles
Editorial Staff
Marlene Canter
Barbara Schadlow
Kathy Winberry

© 1994 Lee Canter & Associates
P.O. Box 2113, Santa Monica, CA 90407-2113
800-262-4347   310-395-3221

Printed in the United States of America
First printing December 1993

97 96 95 94   10 9 8 7 6 5 4 3 2

ISBN #0-939007-73-8

The Morning Rush
—Everyone's in a Hurry

Has anyone seen my gym shorts?

I can't take out the trash—I'll be late for school.

"There's no milk for my cereal?"

"Has anyone seen my book report? I can't find it!"

Why does Jason always get to use the bathroom first? It's not fair.

"Please, Mom, let me sleep just five more minutes."

Sound familiar?

Are your mornings chaotic, rushed, frantic, noisy and disorganized? Do your children oversleep, fight over the bathroom, scramble to get to the bus on time? Are you always running late because wardrobe choices, misplaced homework and food preparation slow you down?

If you're ready to put a stop to this morning madness, we've got some suggestions to make every morning the perfect start to a wonderful day.

Parents Want to Know
Questions & Answers

The hectic pace of morning is familiar to everyone. As parents we know it's important to send our children off feeling happy, secure and content. But problems sometimes arise that can cast an "anything but rosy" glow on the day.

Here are some common concerns of parents just like you.

Q At what age should I expect my child to get himself up in the morning?

ANSWER: You know your child best. Some children are ready to get themselves up by age four or five. Others may not be ready until seven or eight. By age nine, however, your child should be able to awaken to your morning call or the beckoning blast of an alarm clock. (See page 24 for specific tips to wake up your morning "sleepyheads.")

Q My ten-year-old daughter and I argue every morning about what she should wear to school. Help!

ANSWER: Avoid these morning battles by having your daughter choose her school outfit the night before. Although you may sometimes question her fashion choices, let her choose outfits she is comfortable wearing as long as they fit your personal standards, the school's guidelines, and are appropriate for the weather. Hint: Make these clothing discussions part of your nightly routine. Get your child prepared for the following day by discussing tomorrow's weather and any activities that might require specific clothing. When your child wakes up, she will have a headstart on the upcoming day.

Q I'm a single working mother. Is it possible to get my toddler ready to take to the babysitter and my six-year-old son ready for school and get myself ready for work without going crazy? How?

ANSWER: Although it seems like a huge task, it can be done. The key is planning and organization. Make a list of everything that must be done before you leave for work—and then do as much as possible the night before. Your nightly routine might include the following: packing your toddler's bag; helping your son lay out his school clothes; putting everything you'll need tomorrow (keys, purse, briefcase, jacket, lunchbox, umbrella) in a convenient location; preparing lunches; deciding on a quick, nutritious breakfast for the following morning and getting as much ready as possible; bathing your children; putting your toddler to bed in an outfit that is suitable for him to wear to the babysitter's in the morning; choosing your own clothes for the following day. In the morning get yourself ready first. If possible, don't wake the children until you're dressed and coifed.

Q My daughter can be a real slowpoke in the morning. Should I let her watch TV while eating her breakfast?

ANSWER: If your daughter enjoys watching morning TV programs, make TV a privilege she earns for getting ready on time in the morning. Say, "If you get up on time, get dressed, comb your hair and make your bed by 7:30, then you can watch your favorite TV program while eating your breakfast. You must put your breakfast dishes in the sink, have your teeth brushed and your school materials ready by the time the bus arrives at 8:15. There will be no morning TV if you can't keep to this schedule." Be specific about your child's morning routine. Don't give into your daughter's pleadings and let her watch TV if she doesn't fulfill her morning duties.

Q I get tired of yelling at my son to get up in the morning. Isn't there a better way?

ANSWER: Yelling isn't the way to rouse your son from his bed. Consider these wake-up alternatives: Place a clock radio in your son's bedroom and let him wake up to the sounds of his favorite music. Or record your child's favorite morning record ("Zippity Do Dah" or "Good Morning to You") or your own personal morning greeting on a cassette tape and turn it on at wake-up time. You might also consider waking your son with a gentle back rub and a warm hug. Note: Make sure your child is getting enough sleep. He may have a difficult time getting up if he hasn't had adequate rest.

Q My child's bedroom looks like a disaster area in the morning. Should I have him tidy it up before going to school?

ANSWER: That's up to you. Some parents believe a child's room is his own domain. If you do, then the state of disarray in your son's bedroom is his concern—not yours. If you want it tidy but realize that morning isn't the best time for getting the job done, simply close the door and put off bedroom clean-up until after school or before bedtime. If you can't live with the morning mess, then help your son get organized. Make sure he has adequate

boxes for toys. Introduce your son to the hanger, the dresser and the hamper. Explain that clean clothes should be hung up or neatly stored in the dresser. Dirty clothes belong in one place—the hamper. Teach your son how to make his bed. Some children don't comply with a parent's clean-up expectations simply because they lack the skills. Motivate your child to keep his room clean by giving him stars on his Good Morning Chart (pages 37-38).

Q My wife and I both work. We're always on the phone in the morning arranging rides to Little League games, dance lessons, doctor's appointments and friend's homes. This morning confusion doesn't put any of us in a happy frame of mind. Can you help?

ANSWER: A calendar is the answer to your dilemma. Hold a family meeting (preferably on the weekend) to discuss upcoming events, appointments and errands that will require transportation. Record each event on a master calendar. Then designate family drivers or arrange to carpool with friends. Jot down all information on the calendar. Every evening scan the "command post calendar" as a reminder of the next day's after-school plans.

The Morning *Rush* Hour

Weekday mornings can be very hectic. There's so much to do and so little time to do it. Yet some families manage to have peaceful, organized, on-time mornings. How do they do it? It's really simple.

These families:

- plan their mornings,
- share responsibilities, and
- allow adequate time to get ready.

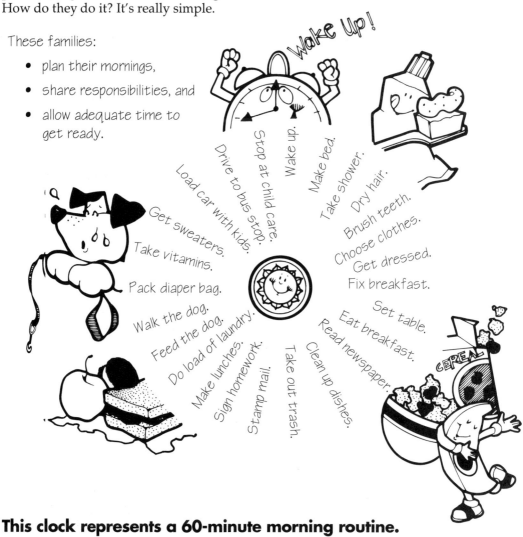

Wake Up!

Wake up.
Make bed.
Take shower.
Dry hair.
Brush teeth.
Choose clothes.
Get dressed.
Fix breakfast.
Set table.
Eat breakfast.
Read newspaper.
Clean up dishes.
Take out trash.
Stamp mail.
Sign homework.
Make lunches.
Do load of laundry.
Feed the dog.
Walk the dog.
Pack diaper bag.
Take vitamins.
Get sweaters.
Load car with kids.
Drive to bus stop.
Stop at child care.

This clock represents a 60-minute morning routine.

As you can see, a family on this schedule has set quite a hectic pace for itself. Even a small problem or a minor interruption can have a domino effect on the whole morning. The result? Everyone gets behind schedule, nerves are frayed, tempers flare, and the morning becomes an unpleasant start to the day. What's the answer? Always expect the unexpected!

You may not think that a lost shoe or an outdated quart of milk could wreak havoc in a household, but little problems can pile up to create one gigantic disaster.

Look at this list of morning setbacks. Separately, each problem doesn't seem too threatening. But imagine a morning with two, three or even more setbacks. Not a pretty picture. Not a happy household.

Morning Setback	Time Lost
• Someone oversleeps	10 minutes
• You can't decide what to wear	5 minutes
• Your son can't find his other shoe	5 minutes searching for shoe
• There's no milk for breakfast cereal	5 minutes preparing another breakfast that doesn't require milk
• Oops! No lunch bags?	5 minutes looking for an alternative lunch sack
• You suddenly remember your child's afternoon dental appointment	10 minutes on telephone rescheduling afternoon meeting
• "Does the dog have fresh water?"	5 minutes (3 minutes arguing about who's responsible for the dog and 2 minutes doing the job)
• "I need to wear my Brownie uniform"	10 minutes (5 minutes searching for the uniform and 5 minutes ironing it)
• "I can't find my homework!"	10 minutes (2 minutes reminding your child to be more responsible for homework and 8 minutes on a homework scavenger hunt)
• You can't find your car keys	5 minutes frantically searching
• "Oh no, I forgot. It's trash day!"	5 minutes taking out the trash cans (15 minutes if you spill on yourself and need to change your clothes)

An ounce of prevention. . .

Problems and interruptions will happen, but they don't need to put your household into a panic—not if you're prepared and organized.

The following pages will explain how your family can work together to minimize these setbacks by planning ahead. This 3-step Morning Routine Plan will have your family solving its morning problems in no time.

Are you ready? Let's get started.

1 Hold a family meeting.

To solve morning problems, your family must work together as a team to pinpoint exactly what's going wrong and to find solutions. A family meeting is the perfect way to get everyone involved.

How to Start

Choose a time when all family members can meet. (The weekend—when the problems of the week are still fresh in everyone's minds—is usually the best time to hold a discussion.) Wherever the meeting is held, it should be easy for everyone to talk to one another and share ideas without interruptions or distractions. Turn off the TV and stereo, get out paper and pencil, and let the meeting begin.

What to Say

Start the meeting by explaining that the family has a problem with its morning routine: It isn't running smoothly. Explain that when problems occur tempers flare, everyone gets behind schedule, and the day is likely to begin on an unhappy note. The solution? The family needs to work together on a plan to make every morning run smoothly.

You might say:

"We have a problem that needs to be solved. As you probably know, our mornings have not been running very smoothly. And when our mornings don't run smoothly, we sometimes fight with one another, get angry and say hurtful things. We need to find out what's going wrong so that we can have good mornings every day.

This problem cannot be solved by just one person. We all need to work together. That's why we're having this meeting today."

STEP **Morning Routine Plan**

2 Pinpoint the problems.

Start by reviewing an average morning in your household. You might say:

> "Every morning of the week we follow a routine—we get up, wash, brush teeth, comb hair, get dressed, eat breakfast, do morning jobs (clean up dishes, make lunches, take out the trash, feed the cat, etc.), gather what we need for the day (lunch, backpack, homework) and leave for school or work."

Then ask family members to pinpoint the problems that are occurring. (Write them on the Morning Problems List on page 35.) You might say:

> "Sometimes problems come up that stop our mornings from running smoothly. To find out what these problems are, let's go through each step of our morning routine and talk about what's causing us to be late or to get upset."

If your children have difficulty pinpointing their problems, use the lists on the next two pages to help get them started.

Read through the following questions.

> "Does anyone have a problem getting up in the morning? What is the problem?"

✎ Write problems on list.

> "Does anyone have a problem getting dressed on time? What is the problem?"

✎ Write problems on list.

> "Any problems getting ready— washing, combing hair, etc.? What is the problem?"

✎ Write problems on list.

> "Do problems ever occur at breakfast? What is the problem?"

✎ Write problems on list.

> "Does anyone have a problem with morning jobs or chores? What is the problem?"

✎ Write problems on list.

> "Any problems gathering things for school, daycare, work? What is the problem?"

✎ Write problems on list.

Common Morning Problems

Getting up on time.

___ I oversleep.

___ I'm too tired to get up in the morning.

___ Mom or Dad doesn't wake me up early enough.

___ I don't hear the alarm.

Getting washed and groomed.

___ I can't get washed up because someone else is always using the bathroom.

___ My brother (sister) takes too much time in the bathroom.

___ There isn't enough hot water left for me to take a shower or bath in the morning.

___ My hair only looks good if I wash it, and there's not enough time in the morning to wash my hair.

Getting dressed on time.

___ I can't decide what to wear.

___ I don't have clean underwear.

___ All my clothes are in the dirty laundry.

___ My skirt (blouse, shirt, dress, uniform) needs to be ironed.

___ I can't find my shoes.

___ I have trouble getting myself dressed (shoes tied, dress buttoned).

Problems at breakfast—preparation, eating, cleaning up.

___ There's nothing to eat for breakfast.

___ There's no milk (juice, cereal, bread for toast, etc.).

___ I don't like to eat breakfast.

___ I don't have time to eat breakfast.

___ Mom is always late making breakfast.

___ I like to watch TV while eating breakfast, but Dad says I dawdle.

___ I don't have time to clean off the breakfast table.

Problems with lunches.

___ There's no bread to make a sandwich for my lunch.

___ There aren't any lunch bags (sandwich bags) for my lunch.

___ I can't find my thermos.

___ Dad doesn't have the right change for my lunch money.

___ I don't like what we have.

___ I don't have time to make my lunch.

Completing morning chores.

___ I don't have time to make my bed (clean my room) before school.

___ There isn't enough time to feed the cat (take out trash, pack lunch, etc.).

___ I always just forget to do it.

___ It's not fair. I have to do all the jobs. (Sibling) doesn't have to do anything.

Gathering materials for the day.

___ I can't find my backpack (homework, library book, science project, sweater, umbrella, boots).

___ I need a parent signature on this field-trip form and I can't find a pen.

___ I need a folder for my book report.

___ I need money for a school project.

Leaving the house on time.

___ Mom can't find her car keys.

___ I'm always late for the bus (car pool).

___ I always forget something and have to go back to get it.

At the end of your discussion, the
Morning Problems List might look
something like this.

Morning Problems LIST

☑ _Too tired to get up._   _JS_
   Morning problem   For whom?

☑ _Clothes aren't clean._   _JS, RS_
   Morning problem   For whom?

☑ _Can't get into bathroom._   _JS_
   Morning problem   For whom?

☑ _Too many morning jobs._   _RS_
   Morning problem   For whom?

☑ _Not enough time to eat._   _JS, RS_
   Morning problem   For whom?

☑ _Can't find homework._   _JS_
   Morning problem   For whom?

☐ _____   _____
   Morning problem   For whom?

☐ _____   _____
   Morning problem   For whom?

☐ _____   _____
   Morning problem   For whom?

☐ _____   _____
   Morning problem   For whom?

☐ _____   _____
   Morning problem   For whom?

☐ _____   _____
   Morning problem   For whom?

☐ _____   _____
   Morning problem   For whom?

☐ _____   _____
   Morning problem   For whom?

Now you're ready to begin solving
these problems!

3 Hold a problem-solving meeting.

By the end of Step #2, you will probably have filled your Morning Problems List with a number of issues that were raised. Now that you've identified the problems you have to deal with, you can begin solving them.

Problem-solving doesn't have to be complicated. It is a very organized process that will take you through these steps:

1. Select the problem(s) you will focus on.

2. Look at what you are doing now that isn't working.

3. Talk about what could be done differently that might stop the problem.

4. Choose the plan you think will work the best.

5. Try the plan for a week.

6. At the end of the week decide how the plan is working.

Gather these materials for your problem-solving meeting:

- Your completed "Morning Problems" List (pages 35-36)

- 6-Step Problem-Solving Guide (pages 39-40)

- "Prescription for a Good Morning" cards (pages 43-44)

- P.S. I Love You Coupons (pages 45-46)

NOTE: Your problem-solving meeting may go more smoothly if you already have in mind some helpful solutions to share. On pages 23-31 you will find suggestions and tips for specific "morning rush" problems. Although you may not find answers to all of your family's problems, you may discover new ways to streamline and improve your morning routine.

Suggestions and Tips:

Your Problem-Solving Meeting

1 Select a problem on which you will focus.

As a family, decide which problems are causing the biggest hassles in the morning. Don't try to solve more than one or two problems per person at this first meeting. Overhauling your family's morning routine is best accomplished in small steps. Refer to your completed Morning Problems List as you decide which problems should be dealt with first.

For example:

Parent: Of the problems you mentioned before, what do you think is your biggest problem in the morning? Which one causes you the most trouble?

Child: I never know what to wear. I can't decide.

2 Look at what you are doing now that isn't working.

Before you can plan a better way to do something, you first need to take a look at what you are doing now that isn't working.

For example:

Parent: Why do you think it takes you so long to choose the clothes you want to wear?

Child: Well, after I wash up and brush my teeth, I come into my bedroom and open the closet. Then I look for something I like to wear. Sometimes my favorite clothes aren't clean or are wrinkled from being in the dryer and then I have a hard time making up my mind. Sometimes I try on lots of different outfits until I find one I want to wear.

3 | Talk about what could be done differently that might stop the problem.

Encourage your children to come up with their own solutions. They will be more likely to make changes if they've had some part in making the decision.

For example:

Parent: What could you do differently that might help you get dressed more quickly?

Child: I suppose I could get up earlier, but I have a hard enough time getting up now. Or I could have you pick out something for me to wear, but sometimes you choose stuff I don't like very much.

Parent: Is there a better time for you to pick out your school clothes?

Child: I guess I could pick them out before I go to bed. Then if something needed ironing, there'd be time to do it at night.

4 | Together choose the plan you think will work the best.

Guide your child in choosing a plan of action that seems most appropriate—and the most likely to succeed. Remember to look over the suggestions and tips on pages 24-31 for additional ideas if needed.

For example:

Parent: Okay. You've given me three ideas that might help solve this problem. You've said that in order to get dressed on time you could get up earlier, have me choose your clothes, or you could decide what to wear the night before. Which plan do you think might work the best?

Child: I think I'd like to pick out my clothes the night before.

5 Try the plan for a week.

By designating a time limit, your family can try a plan knowing you have the opportunity to stop and change things if they're not working out.

For example:

Parent: I think that's a great decision. Let's try it for a week. Every night before you go to bed, you will pick out what you're going to wear to school the next day, including underwear, shoes and socks. To save even more time, you could lay everything out on your dresser. How does that sound?

Child: I think I could do that.

Parent: Great! Let's write this plan on one of these "Prescription for a Good Morning" cards. Each morning that you get dressed on time, I'll put a star on the back of this card. And when you have five stars, I'll give you a special P.S. I Love You Coupon.

6 At the end of the week, decide how the plan is working.

If the problem seems to be solved, and the morning routine is going smoother, the solution worked. Continue tracking your child's progress on the back of the prescription card for several weeks, handing out P.S. I Love You Coupons for special privileges.

If the plan is not working, try another solution. Try one of the other plans you came up with, or go through the problem-solving process again. Evaluate why this plan didn't work and share ideas for what might work better. Choose a plan and try it.

> Repeat this process for each problem. Soon family members will begin problem-solving on their own.

Motivate Your Child!

Once you've decided on a plan, the next step is putting these solutions into practice. Sometimes it's difficult to change old habits, but with praise and encouragement your children should be able to make the transition.

Use the "Good Morning" tracking charts on pages 37-38 to give your child that extra incentive to get on track and stay on track.

Here's what to do:

Tell your child that each day he or she gets up on time (specify the behavior you want to pinpoint) a sun or sticker will be put on the chart.

When you reach a goal of a certain number of suns a reward will be earned. Keep in mind: The younger the child, the fewer the number of suns should be needed to earn the reward.

A praiseworthy tip to parents

Your words of praise, more than anything else, will motivate your child to get up and be ready on time in the morning. Make a point of noticing the efforts your child makes, and saying something positive about them.

"You were up and dressed today even before I came in to check on you. Great job! Now you have some extra time to enjoy your breakfast without rushing."

Don't underestimate the power of your praise. It can make all the difference in the world.

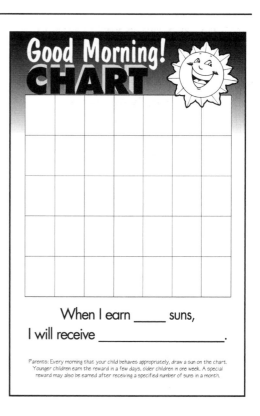

Good Morning! CHART

When I earn _____ suns,
I will receive _____.

Parents: Every morning that your child behaves appropriately, draw a sun on the chart. Younger children earn the reward in a few days, older children in one week. A special reward may also be earned after receiving a specified number of suns in a month.

If Problems Persist . . .

✔ You've pinpointed your family's problems in the morning.

✔ You've tried different plans of action to solve these problems.

✔ You've given lots of praise for good effort—but mornings are still hectic and unpleasant!

If the actions you have taken have not done the trick, and you find yourself struggling with your child each morning, it's time to use the Morning Contract (see page 41).

What is a Morning Contract?

This contract is a written agreement between you and your child that states:

1) The morning rule your child must follow.

2) The specific reward your child will receive for following the morning rule.

3) The privileges that will be taken away if your child chooses not to follow the rule.

Rules

Meet with your child to discuss the specific problem. Explain that together you will develop a new rule in the house. Depending on the problem your child is having with his or her morning routine, the new rule may be:

___ Get up at the designated time.

___ Get washed, dressed and ready for school without help.

___ Set aside enough time for breakfast.

___ Clean up room.

___ Gather belongings for school (lunch, homework, books) the night before and leave by door.

___ Complete chores before leaving home.

___ Other _____

Say to your child, for example:

"Sarah, we've tried several different ideas to help us have smoother running mornings, but unfortunately we're still having problems. I've come up with a different idea that I think will help you. First, we're going to have a new morning rule. The new rule is: You will be dressed and ready for breakfast at 7:30 each morning."

Write the new rule on the Morning Contract (pages 41-42).

Rewards

Decide how you will reward your child for following the rule. For example, your child may:

___ Earn a sticker or star on the Good Morning Chart. (See page 37.)

___ Be awarded a P.S. I Love You Coupon.

___ Be given a special award.

___ Participate in a special activity after school.

___ Have a "special dress day" to wear whatever he or she wants.

___ Watch morning TV until it's time to leave if he or she gets ready quickly.

___ Watch a favorite video with Mom and Dad.

___ Other _____

Say to your child, for example:

"I know you can follow this rule, Sarah. And to let you how much I appreciate it, every time that you are at the table ready to eat at 7:30 you will earn a star on the Good Morning Chart. When you have five stars we'll go out to lunch together. How does that sound?"

Consequences

Decide what privilege or activity you will take away if your child does not follow the new rule. For example, your child might:

___ Go to his or her room after school for as many minutes as he or she was late getting out of bed in the morning.

___ Lose the privilege of playing with friends after school.

___ Lose the privilege of playing video games until morning responsibilities are completed on time.

___ Lose telephone privileges if fighting continues with siblings.

___ Stay in room until completely dressed.

___ Other _____

Say to your child, for example:

"If you don't choose to follow this rule, you'll lose a privilege. That means each day that you are not at the breakfast table on time you will lose phone privileges for the rest of the day."

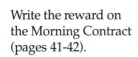

Write the reward on the Morning Contract (pages 41–42).

Write the consequence on the Morning Contract (pages 41–42).

Sign it and date it.

Once the contract is completed, sign and date it. Then post it on a cupboard, bulletin board or the refrigerator door.

MORNING CONTRACT

The new rule in our house will be:

Dressed & ready for breakfast at 7:30.
New Rule

If _____ *Sarah* _____
Child's Name

does follow the rule,

she will earn a star on
Reward

the Good Morning Chart.

If _____ *Sarah* _____
Child's Name

does not follow the rule,

she will lose phone privileges
Consequence

for the rest of the day.

_____
Parent's Signature

_____
Child's Signature

_____
Date

Remember, you must be consistent.

- If your child breaks the rule, you must follow through with the consequence.
- If your child follows the rules, you must provide the reward.
- Praise your child whenever he or she follows the rule.

Suggestions & Tips
for Successful Mornings

The following pages contain lots of ideas for organizing your morning routine. Scan these pages for ways to make your morning run more smoothly. Use these suggestions in your problem-solving meetings.

Suggestions & Tips for
Waking Up on Time

Wake up, you sleepyheads!

Try these suggestions for getting your family out of bed on time.

- [ ] Make sure your child is getting enough sleep. Change your child's bedtime if he or she isn't getting adequate rest.

- [ ] Give your child an alarm clock and teach him or her how to use it.

- [ ] Place a clock radio in your child's bedroom so that she may wake up to the sounds of her favorite music.

- [ ] Record your child's favorite song or a personal morning greeting from you on a cassette tape and turn it on at wake-up time.

- [ ] Wake your child with a gentle back rub and a warm hug. It's a great way to start the day.

- [ ] Provide lots of praise and enthusiasm when your child gets up without prodding. It's important to reinforce the positive behavior so that your child will be more likely to repeat it.

- [ ] Use the Good Morning Chart on page 37 to track your child's wake-up routine. Each morning your child gets up on time, put a check (or a sticker) on the chart. When your child has received a specific number of checks (5, 10 or more), reward your child with a P.S. I Love You Coupon. (See page 45.)

What's one of the first things your child should see in the morning? A smile on your face! Start your child's day on a positive note, and the chances are good that the hours that follow will be more pleasant—for the both of you. You may be rushed and harried yourself, but when you take the time to give a morning smile, you'll find yourself receiving one too!

Suggestions & Tips for
Sharing the Bathroom

Hurry up. I've got to use the bathroom too.

Sharing a bathroom during morning rush hour is a necessity in most households, but it doesn't have to be a problem. Keep your family on schedule with these bathroom suggestions:

☐ Too many people and not enough time or hot water? Have some family members take their baths or showers the night before. Rotate the schedule so it's fair for everyone.

☐ Stagger wake-up times, especially in one-bathroom households.

☐ Make a schedule for using the bathroom and post it on the bathroom door.

☐ Place a wind-up timer or battery-operated wall clock in the bathroom to keep everyone on schedule.

☐ Confine bathroom time to "water activities only"—washing up, using the toilet, brushing teeth, etc.

☐ Place a mirror in each bedroom so that your children can get dressed, comb their hair and complete the rest of their morning preparations outside of the bathroom.

☐ Make your bathroom clean-up expectations clear. "When you leave the bathroom, the sink should be clean, towels should be hung up, dirty clothes in the hamper, and the toilet lid should be down."

♥ Remember to thank everyone concerned for their cooperation in sharing the bathroom. Small gifts now and then such as bubble bath, a new comb or toothbrush are great ways to say "I appreciate the way you help us all work together."

Suggestions & Tips for
Getting Dressed on Time

The easiest way to put an end to morning battles over clothes is to plan what to wear the night before. Help your child make clothing choices by discussing the weather and your child's plans for the upcoming day. Is a cold, winter breeze in tomorrow's forecast? Don't forget a warm sweater or jacket! Dance class tomorrow? Better put out the tutu and toe shoes. Little League practice? Get the cleats out of the closet!

Here are some more suggestions to help your family get dressed in record time.

☐ Have everyone make their clothing choices the night before.

☐ Don't forget to check on clean clothes, underwear and socks. Precious morning time can be lost waiting for clothes to dry in the dryer.

☐ When putting away clean laundry, match up your child's outfits on hangers or in drawers (blue print shirt, blue shorts and blue socks—all together).

☐ If your child is always losing a shoe, purchase an inexpensive hanging storage rack for shoes. Tack it to the back of the bedroom door or inside the closet. Give your child a star on the Good Morning Chart (page 37) each time he puts both shoes in the storage rack.

☐ Have your child tie the shoelaces from both shoes together when removing shoes. Then place the shoes at the foot of the bed. Getting into this routine will pay off in a week or two.

> What do you mean you don't have anything to wear?

☐ Socks lost in the laundry? When purchasing socks, buy two pairs of the same color. Then if one gets lost, you've still got a spare.

☐ Put a lost and found box in the laundry room. Every time a stray article of clothing is found, place it in the lost and found.

☐ Jot down missing articles on a notepad. That evening have your child go on an afterschool scavenger hunt looking for the missing articles. Reward your child's efforts with a P.S. I Love You Coupon. (See page 45.)

☐ Does your child dawdle when dressing or need a little extra morning motivation? Set a timer for 3-5 minutes. If she gets dressed before the timer goes off, she earns a star on her Good Morning Chart.

♥ When you tiptoe into your child's room late at night for a last-minute peek, and see her clothes laid out, ready for the next day, place a little "love note" on her sweater or jeans: "Thank you for helping get the mornings off to a great start!"

Suggestions & Tips for
Younger Children Getting Dressed by Themselves

Does your younger child have problems getting dressed? It's difficult enough to get older children ready for the day. Little ones, however hard they may try, may succeed only in trying your patience! Both of you need all the help you can get. Try these suggestions, and remember that morning rush hours were not designed with toddlers in mind. Stay calm and praise your child for trying even though he or she may fall short of your expectations.

Mommy, I can't tie my shoe.

- ☐ If your child is under the age of six, stay away from clothes with buttons. T-shirts and pull-on pants are the fastest and easiest clothes for a child to put on.

- ☐ Slip-on shoes and footwear with velcro fasteners are the easiest for children to put on. Avoid laces before age six.

- ☐ Tennies on the wrong feet? Draw an arrow pointing toward the big toe on the sole of each shoe.

- ☐ Does your child put shirts, pants, shorts, or underwear on backwards? With a permanent marker, write your child's initial on the front of the garment. Then demonstrate that this mark always "goes on the side with the toes." (It's also a great way to identify which garments belong to which family members.)

- ☐ Help your child place his or her clothes out the night before. Talk together about what would be good to wear the next day, and why. Your child will be less likely to balk at the day's clothing selection if he or she has a part in choosing.

♥ Young children need lots of praise, hugs and kisses for doing "big kid" things like getting themselves dressed. It's a great opportunity for some special morning words that will send your children off feeling good about themselves.

Suggestions & Tips for
Breakfast

There's no milk for my cereal!

Is breakfast time a problem at your house? Do your children dawdle or complain about "the same old boring breakfast"? Is your morning meal too rushed to enjoy? Don't skip breakfast or allow your children to miss this important meal. Your children need a nutritious breakfast in the morning. Without proper nourishment, your child will be unable to concentrate on schoolwork or can become irritable and fussy with classmates and friends.

Keep your kitchen stocked with a variety of healthy breakfast foods including cereals, fruits, juices, breads, yogurt, etc. But you don't have to limit your family to traditional breakfast foods only. Your breakfast menu can include any food that your family finds appealing and that provides adequate nutrition. If leftover lasagna, a roll and milk sounds appealing, fire up the microwave and pass the pasta.

Here are ways to manage a healthy morning meal without a lot of fuss.

☐ Get everything ready the night before. Set the table, mix up batter, set out the cereal boxes, and stir up some juice. Enlist the help of your children with this project.

☐ Watching TV will only make a slow eater slower. Turn on the radio instead or, better yet, talk about the upcoming day.

☐ Place a 5-minute egg timer by your child's plate. Challenge your child to finish her meal just as the time runs out. (Hint: Check your children's games for time-keeping devices.)

☐ Store single-serving leftovers in microwavable dishes or on paper plates covered with plastic wrap. Next morning, just pop in the microwave for a hearty, nutritious morning meal.

☐ Make extra pancakes, waffles, French toast, and muffins on the weekend. Store serving-size portions in small freezer bags. Microwave for a quick breakfast favorite.

☐ Cleanup doesn't have to be an over-whelming problem. Make sure that everyone knows exactly what they are expected to do with dirty dishes. Then expect them to follow through. For example: Clear the table of your own dishes. Rinse your dishes and put in the dishwasher or leave to soak in the sink. Wipe up your place at the table. The key to clean-up success is clarifying your expectations.

♡ A special morning treat can be a great morning motivator. Say to your child(ren), "Everyone who's at breakfast on time tomorrow will enjoy a special surprise!" The treat can be as simple as a muffin or as unexpected as a coffee cake with a "frosting message" ("Have a great day!") on top. You know what your children like—go for it!

Suggestions & Tips for
Making Lunches

> I don't want another peanut butter and jelly sandwich!

A healthy breakfast keeps your family going during the morning hours, but they need to refuel at lunch to sustain their concentration and attentiveness until dinner time. The morning rush sometimes prevents us from packing nutritious lunches for the family, and buying a healthful lunch isn't always an option. Once again, preparation can save the day. If you know you are going to be making lunches everyday, make sure to buy enough lunch foods for the entire week. There's nothing more frustrating than scrambling for lunch ingredients on a busy morning.

Try these ideas for creating appetizing meals for your "brown baggers."

☐ Pack as much of the lunch as possible the night before. Store the sack in the refrigerator and attach a Post-it™ note listing any morning additions to the sack—chips, banana, etc.

☐ Vary your sandwich-making ingredients. Use hamburger and hot dog buns, croissants, bagels, pita bread, crackers, dinner rolls, or rice cakes instead of bread. The variety will keep your children interested and eating!

☐ Veggies make excellent lunch treats. Keep carrot and celery sticks crisp until lunch by adding an ice cube to a self-sealing bag before adding the vegetables. For a special treat add a little container of yogurt or salad dressing for dipping.

☐ Keep drinks cold by freezing drink or fruit-juice boxes. Wrap with aluminum foil to avoid soggy sacks.

☐ Don't be caught short! Keep an extra loaf of bread in the freezer at all times. (An extra jar of peanut butter on the shelf could come in handy, too.)

☐ Lunch doesn't always have to mean a sandwich. Bag your child's lunch ingredients separately (bread sticks, meat and cheese cubes, cherry tomatoes) for eating a la carte.

☐ Save those plastic spoons and send them along for yogurt, puddings and fruit cups.

☐ Add a folded paper towel or two to use as a placemat and napkin.

The more interesting and appealing the lunch, the less likely it will be tossed out or traded in favor of chips and desserts.

♥ Insert a note in your child's lunch bag with a special smile-inspiring message!

Suggestions & Tips for
Completing Morning Jobs

Is your child responsible for doing household jobs? Most children have certain responsibilities—pet care, bedroom clean-up, meal duties. But many children balk at doing their chores in the morning, saying they don't have time, or that completing chores will make them late. If your children's household responsibilities include some "morning musts," try these ideas:

> I don't have time to take out the trash before I leave. I'll do it tonight.

☐ Put a morning jobs checklist on the refrigerator. Place a check mark beside each job as it is completed. Scan the list before the family leaves to make sure that all jobs are completed.

☐ Does your child complain that he or she doesn't have enough time in the morning to complete household jobs? Set the wake-up alarm 10 minutes earlier. This may be just the incentive for youngsters to work a little faster or organize their schedules more wisely.

☐ Bedroom a mess? Make bedroom clean-up part of your child's nightly routine—toys put away, dirty clothes in the hamper, books on the shelf. If the room is shipshape at bedtime, the only job for morning will be making the bed.

☐ If chores are not completed in the morning, take away an after-school privilege for the day (no telephone, no video games, no playing with friends).

☐ Motivate your child to complete chores and keep bedroom clean by awarding stars on his/her Good Morning Chart when tasks are completed.

☐ Play "Beat the Clock." Set the oven timer for 10 minutes (or however long it will take to complete morning chores). If your child can complete all morning jobs before the timer buzzes, he earns a special award.

☐ Morning jobs often ask a lot of your child because they need to be taken care of in the middle of the morning rush. Make sure the jobs are fairly distributed and if appropriate rotate the more demanding ones.

♥
"Thank you's" are always in order when your child completes a morning job. Put a P.S. I Love You Coupon in your child's lunch to show how much you appreciate the help.

Suggestions & Tips for
Getting Ready to Leave on Time

Has anyone seen my homework?

I can't find my car keys!

Do these grievances sound familiar? The answer to these morning problems is organization. When your family is organized, the last-minute rush to find misplaced items and get out the door on time will be history.

Try these ideas for keeping track of important morning items:

☐ Designate a special place (called the "Drop Spot") for your child to place all important belongings that must go to school (or to the babysitter or daycare) in the morning. Choose a location that is on the path he/she takes every morning leaving the house.

☐ Have your child decorate a large box in which to store his or her homework, library and school books, notebook, backpack, etc. Keep the box at the foot of your child's bed. Personalize this box with a "Drop Spot" label.

☐ Purchase a brightly colored 9" x 12" clasp envelope. Encourage your child to keep it in his or her backpack for transporting important notes and papers between home and school. Then get into the habit of asking your child if these are any "special deliveries" in the envelope.

☐ Attention parents: Always locate your own morning-rush items (keys, briefcase, mail, etc.) before going to bed.

☐ Choose your own "Drop Spot" too. Get in the habit of always placing your keys, wallet, purse, diaper bag— anything you'll need to take with you in the morning—in this spot.

☐ Make several duplicate sets of keys— for the car and for the house. Place one set in the family "Drop Spot" box. Place another set in your family's first aid box.

♥ Be good to yourself. Harried mornings are harder on you than anyone else. Try getting up fifteen minutes early for some quiet time alone. Some peaceful moments with the newspaper and your breakfast will help you face the day with calmness and a positive outlook.

How to Speak So Your Child Will Listen

> I might as well be talking to myself!

Does your child tune you out, ignore you, or argue with you when you ask him or her to get ready in the morning (or anything else, for that matter)? If this is typical in your home it may have a lot to do with the way you are speaking to your child.

Parents who are successful in encouraging better behavior speak to their children in a clear, direct and firm manner that leaves no doubt about what is expected.

Parents who are ignored or argued with often speak in a way that is either wishy washy or hostile.

Do any of these comments sound familiar?

"How many times do I have to tell you to get out of bed?"

"Please get downstairs and eat your breakfast. The bus will be here in ten minutes."

"It's time to leave and the dog still hasn't been taken out."

Chances are you've said things like these many times. Most parents have. But what do statements like these really say to your child? Look at each one carefully and you will see that they either ask pointless questions, beg, or make an obvious statement of fact. They do not let the child know without a doubt that you expect him to get out of bed now, go to breakfast now, take care of the dog or choose clothes the night before. Wishy-washy statements don't let your child know that your words are to be taken seriously—that you mean business.

They make it easy for your child to ignore you.

And what about comments like these?

"I should know better than to expect you to get out of bed by yourself on time."

"I've had it with dealing with this dog. You're too irresponsible to take care of him—maybe it's time to take him to the pound."

"That's it. You can just stay home this weekend."

What do these all-too-common remarks say to a child? Put-downs, meaningless threats and off-the-wall punishments, because they are emotional and often inappropriate, are an invitation to challenge and anger. Because they disregard a child's feelings they send a message to the child that says "I don't like you." Hostile responses tear down a child's self-esteem and are ultimately damaging. The words your child hears from you will become the way he or she feels about himself or herself.

Learn to speak so your child will listen.

Don't beg. Don't get angry. Don't become exasperated. Instead, when making a request of your child, be calm and use direct statements that send your child this message: "This is what I expect you to do."

"Marie, get out of bed now."

"Danny, breakfast is on the table. I want you down here now."

"Amanda, take the dog out for her walk."

Confident, clear and direct statements get results.

And if your child argues?

Above all, don't argue back. Do not get involved in a discussion. It will get you nowhere. The following scene illustrates this point:

Parent: Danny, breakfast is ready.

Child: *(watching TV)* I'm not hungry now. Just let me me finish this cartoon, please?

Parent: Danny, I don't think you need cartoons in the morning every day, do you? Now come on in and eat.

Child: I said I'm not hungry.

Parent: You know you'll be hungry later. Please turn off that TV and come to the table.

Child: I promise I'll be there in just a few minutes, OK?

Parent: Oh sure. Would you eat your cereal if I bring it in there?

What happened here? By arguing the parent has lost control of the situation. Danny's still watching TV. And the parent finally gives in by bringing breakfast to him! Chances are Mom feels angry and manipulated, but figures that at least he's eating. What about tomorrow? She's set herself up for a hassle every morning.

What should you do in a situation like this?

Don't argue. Use the "broken record" technique.

First, very clearly tell your child what you want her to do. If she argues, simply repeat the statement, like a broken record. Do not argue back or even discuss the issue. Repeat your expectation.

For example:

Parent: Danny, breakfast is ready. Come in and sit down.

Child: (watching TV) I'm not hungry now. Just let me me finish this cartoon, please? It's my favorite.

Parent: I understand that you may not feel hungry, but break-fast is ready. I want you to turn off the TV and sit down at the table now.

Child: That's not fair. I don't want to eat and I want to see this show.

Parent: I understand that its an interesting show, Danny, but I want you to turn off the TV and come to the table now.

By staying firm, not arguing, not getting sidetracked, chances are good your child will comply with your request. He or she may grumble and complain, but will probably get up and do as you ask.

If necessary, back up your words with actions.

If, however, after three repetitions of your expectations your child still does not comply, it's time to back up your words with actions and present your child with a clear choice:

Parent: Danny, I expect you to come to the table now. If you choose not to come to the table and eat you will choose to lose TV privileges the rest of the week. The choice is yours.

By giving your child a choice you place responsibility for what happens right where it belongs—squarely on your child's shoulders.

Try these techniques the next time your child balks at fulfilling a responsibility or responding to a request. Just take a deep breath and follow through calmly and confidently. You'll find that this approach does work!

Morning Rush Worksheets

On the following pages you will find the planning sheets, awards and other worksheets that have been referred to throughout this book. Each sheet is 2-sided, so you can use it more than once.

Before using these sheets, you may wish to make additional copies so you will always have plenty of resources close at hand when you need them.

Morning Problems
LIST

☐ _____   _____
Morning problem   For whom?

☐ _____   _____
Morning problem   For whom?

☐ _____   _____
Morning problem   For whom?

☐ _____   _____
Morning problem   For whom?

☐ _____   _____
Morning problem   For whom?

☐ _____   _____
Morning problem   For whom?

☐ _____   _____
Morning problem   For whom?

☐ _____   _____
Morning problem   For whom?

☐ _____   _____
Morning problem   For whom?

☐ _____   _____
Morning problem   For whom?

☐ _____   _____
Morning problem   For whom?

☐ _____   _____
Morning problem   For whom?

☐ _____   _____
Morning problem   For whom?

☐ _____   _____
Morning problem   For whom?

Morning Problems
LIST

☐ _____   _____
Morning problem   For whom?

☐ _____   _____
Morning problem   For whom?

☐ _____   _____
Morning problem   For whom?

☐ _____   _____
Morning problem   For whom?

☐ _____   _____
Morning problem   For whom?

☐ _____   _____
Morning problem   For whom?

☐ _____   _____
Morning problem   For whom?

☐ _____   _____
Morning problem   For whom?

☐ _____   _____
Morning problem   For whom?

☐ _____   _____
Morning problem   For whom?

☐ _____   _____
Morning problem   For whom?

☐ _____   _____
Morning problem   For whom?

☐ _____   _____
Morning problem   For whom?

☐ _____   _____
Morning problem   For whom?

Good Morning! CHART

When I earn _____ suns,

I will receive _____.

Parents: Every morning that your child behaves appropriately, draw a sun on the chart.
Younger children earn the reward in a few days, older children in one week. A special
reward may also be earned after receiving a specified number of suns in a month.

Good Morning! CHART

When I earn _____ suns,
I will receive _____.

Parents: Every morning that your child behaves appropriately, draw a sun on the chart. Younger children earn the reward in a few days, older children in one week. A special reward may also be earned after receiving a specified number of suns in a month.

SIX-STEP PROBLEM-SOLVING GUIDE

1. Identify the problem.

_____

_____

2. What are you doing about this problem now?

_____

_____

3. Discuss what could be done that might stop the problem. Discuss several plans.

_____

_____

_____

_____

4. Choose the plan you think will work best.

5. Try the plan for a week.

6. At the end of the week, decide how the plan is working and if you need to change it.

_____

_____

_____

* If the plan is not working, try another solution.

SIX-STEP PROBLEM-SOLVING GUIDE

1. Identify the problem.

_____

_____

2. What are you doing about this problem now?

_____

_____

3. Discuss what could be done that might stop the problem. Discuss several plans.

_____

_____

_____

_____

4. Choose the plan you think will work best.

5. Try the plan for a week.

6. At the end of the week, decide how the plan is working and if you need to change it.

_____

_____

_____

* If the plan is not working, try another solution.

MORNING CONTRACT

The new rule in our house will be:

_____
New Rule

If _____
Child's Name

does follow the rule,

_____
Reward

_____

If _____
Child's Name

does not follow the rule,

_____
Consequence

_____

_____
Parent's Signature

_____
Child's Signature

_____
Date

MORNING CONTRACT

The new rule in our house will be:

_____
New Rule

If _____
Child's Name

does follow the rule,

_____
Reward

_____

If _____
Child's Name

does not follow the rule,

_____
Consequence

_____

_____
Parent's Signature

_____
Child's Signature

_____
Date

Prescription
for a Good Morning

For: _____

Problem: _____

_____

Solution (Prescription): _____

_____

_____

Turn over to track your success.

Prescription
for a Good Morning

For: _____

Problem: _____

_____

Solution (Prescription): _____

_____

_____

Turn over to track your success.

Prescription
for a Good Morning

Week 1						Your special reward will be:
Week 2						Your special reward will be:
Week 3						Your special reward will be:
Week 4						Your special reward will be:

Each day I follow this prescription, I earn one star.
When I earn 5 stars in a week, I will receive a special reward.

Prescription
for a Good Morning

Week 1						Your special reward will be:
Week 2						Your special reward will be:
Week 3						Your special reward will be:
Week 4						Your special reward will be:

Each day I follow this prescription, I earn one star.
When I earn 5 stars in a week, I will receive a special reward.

Thank You!

♥ P.S. I Love You

Have a great Day!

♥ P.S. I Love You

Great Job!

♥ P.S. I Love You

Super!

♥ P.S. I Love You

Use these coupons to write a caring note to your child
or to present him or her with a special reward.

Thank You!

♥ P.S. I Love You

Have a great Day!

♥ P.S. I Love You

Great Job!

♥ P.S. I Love You

Super!

♥ P.S. I Love You

Use these coupons to write a caring note to your child
or to present him or her with a special reward.

Lee Canter's
Top 10 "Morning Rush" Reminders

Once your Morning Routine plan is underway you'll enjoy calmer, happier, more on-schedule mornings. With continued attention, most of your morning rush problems can remain a thing of the past. Here then are our Top Ten "Morning Rush" Reminders to help you keep things on track and running smoothly. Refer to these reminders from time to time whenever you need a quick refresher!

1 When mornings inevitably get chaotic don't get discouraged! Keep in mind that a multitude of activities go on each morning in a very short timespan. Mornings are tough. You do have a lot to get done, and you can't expect that things will always run on schedule. Take a deep breath, approach your morning routine calmly and confidently—then take action to solve the problems that have arisen.

2 Remember that many "morning rush" problems stem from things that could have been taken care of the night before. Making clothing choices, confirming next-day schedules, doing homework checks, signing notes for school and packing lunches should all be dealt with before going to bed.

3 Some morning problems require family teamwork to solve. When persistent problems cause ongoing headaches, sit down and talk about it. Listen respectfully to the opinions of all concerned and do some family problem solving to arrive at solutions that will benefit everyone.

4 Last-minute morning searches inevitably cause a lot of morning tears and frustration. Organize individual or family "drop spots" where family members can leave things that need to be taken with them the next morning: homework, briefcase, school supplies, toys, sports equipment, keys, etc.

5 Amid the hustle and bustle of busy mornings it's sometimes easy to forget that you're the one in charge. Bottom line, you are the one responsible for getting the household organized–buying the food, getting the laundry done, setting the daily timetable in motion. For the most part, these responsibilities are yours—not your children's. It is worthwhile therefore to take a close look at your own role in the morning rush hour. Review your own activities: what you need to do each morning, how you could organize better, what you could do ahead of time, what responsibilities could be shared. Take a look at the problems carefully—some things you can solve just by taking action on your own.

6 Your praise, more than anything else, will encourage your child to continue to meet your morning expectations. And don't save your praise for perfection—praise improvement, too. Baby steps will turn into giant steps when your appreciation is freely given.

7 Morning arguments don't enhance anyone's day. When you need the cooperation of your child to get something done, state your expectations calmly and clearly. Don't argue. Don't beg. Your child will pay much more attention to your requests when you speak in a firm and caring manner and avoid discussions that aren't getting either of you anywhere.

8 If your child has problems getting up in the morning take a look at what time he or she goes to bed. Your child needs adequate sleep in order to start the day refreshed. A successful morning routine requires an equally successful bedtime routine the night before.

9 As every parent knows, in spite of everything you do, some problems just aren't solved easily. Keep in mind that it's to your benefit, and your child's, to actively help him or her make better behavior choices. A morning contract (as described in this book) will give you the structure you sometimes need to get your child on track.

10 Set a happy tone to the day! The first fifteen minutes of the morning set the tone for the entire day. Greet family members with a smile, a hug and some positive, encouraging words. Everyone should leave the house feeling good about themselves and ready to take on the day.